The Cream of The Kop

The Songs of Liverpool F.C.

by

A. E. Heathcote

D1471977

**Grosvenor House
Publishing Limited**

This book is published by
Grosvenor House Publishing Ltd
28-30 High Street, Guildford, Surrey, GU1 3HY.
www.grosvenorhousepublishing.co.uk

A CIP record for this book
is available from the British Library

ISBN 978-1-906210-41-0

'You'll Never Walk Alone' Words by Oscar Hammerstein ll
and Music by Richard Rodgers

For the fans.
Without you there would be
no songs, no chants, no team and no Liverpool

Introduction

So here it is. The definitive collection of Liverpool songs and chants as sung by you, the fans, from the most famous stand in world football.

With 18 League titles, 12 European trophies and 14 domestic Cup wins Liverpool are the most successful team in British history. But it is not only the team that is famous worldwide.

For so many years now the unwavering belief, fanatical faith and boundless patience have been an example to fans everywhere of just what it really means to be a supporter. Granted, Liverpool fans have more to sing about than most but for a long time now success has been limited. Support, most certainly, has not.

Every week we see individuals or even entire teams booed and derided by their own 'faithful', when times are hard or impatience takes hold. As a football fan I have seen this far too many times throughout the years, but it is a part of modern football that has always been refreshingly absent from Liverpool. One particular night in Istanbul comes immediately to mind...

Whether it be support for the team, an individual player or some interesting facts about the appearance/quality/history/sexual orientation etc of the opposition, Liverpool fans have a song for it.

There are songs within these pages which are proud, moving, nasty or downright hilarious, and all of which paint a fantastic historical portrait of Liverpool Football Club from the perspective of those that make it what it is. The fans.

So please enjoy, but remember; don't take it too seriously. I mean, it's not like it's a matter of life or death. Is it?

'Some people believe football is a matter of life and death, I am very disappointed with that attitude. I can assure you it is much, much more important than that.'

Bill Shankly

You'll Never Walk Alone

You'll Never Walk Alone has been the anthem of Liverpool F.C ever since being played in Merseyside clubs by Gerry and the Pacemakers in 1963. One of the most famous songs of all time it has brought together the club, the players and the fans in times of great joy, as well as times of great tragedy

When you walk through a storm
Hold your head up high
And don't be afraid of the dark
At the end of the storm
Is a golden sky
And the sweet silver song of a lark

Walk on through the wind
Walk on through the rain
Though your dreams be tossed and blown
Walk on, walk on
With hope in your heart
And you'll never walk alone
You'll never walk alone

'There's not one club in Europe with an anthem like You'll Never Walk Alone. There's not one club in the world so united with the fans. I sat there watching the Liverpool fans and they sent shivers down my spine. A mass of 40,000 people became one force behind their team. That's something not many teams have. For that I admire Liverpool more than anything.'

Dutch legend **Johan Cruyff**
after the EC Final in Istanbul

The Irish Rover

Homage to John Houlding, founder of Liverpool F.C

In the year of our Lord eighteen ninety and two
John Houlding went and evicted the Blues
From their Anfield abode on the Walton Breck Road
He was tired of seeing them lose

Year's behind in rent all their money was spent
A bank that held nothing but zero's
But Houlding instead built a team dressed in Red
Liverpool, his Anfield heroes

'If you are first you are first.
If you are second you are nothing.'

Bill Shankly

Thanks To The Shanks

Another song for the greatest of them all

He was born in bonny Scotland
And he played the football game
He came to Liverpool in '59
To help us win again
Then with his mighty Red Army
He marched to victory
He was the legend of his time
Our hero, Bill Shankly

So all say thanks to the Shanks
He never walked alone
Lets sing our song, for all the world
Of this, his Liverpool home

No matter where you come from
No matter who you are
Remember the year of '59
When the Reds, they found a star
And how he shines so brightly
For the boys of Liverpool
Soon the world was about to find
This man was nobody's fool

So all say thanks to the Shanks
He never walked alone
Lets sing our song, for all the world
Of this, his Liverpool home

The man he asked no favours
Just hard work, let's get it right
You can only succeed through dedication
And his men they all saw the light
He gave this town his loyalty
And proved it all by success
So always remember, when we had Bill Shankly
We all knew we had the best

So all say thanks to the Shanks
He never walked alone
Lets sing our song, for all the world
Of this, his Liverpool home
Shankly, Shankly, Shankly, Shankly

'He was the greatest person I know.'

Ron Yeats on Bill Shankly

L – I - V... (Jesus Christ Superstar)

One of the most popular Liverpool songs ever, this has been sung over and over again for more than thirty years

L – I – V

E – R – P

Double O – L

Liverpool F.C

(Repeat as necessary)

'It's there to remind our lads who they're playing for, and to remind the opposition who they're playing against.'

Bill Shankly on the 'This is Anfield' plaque

Billy Liddell (Amore)

Praise for the legendary winger

When he runs down the wing
You can hear the Kop sing
Billy Liddell
When he runs through to score
You can hear the Kop roar
Billy Liddell
La, la, la, la, la, la
La, la, la, la, la, la
Bil-ly Lid-dell

'Bill was so strong it was unbelievable. You couldn't shake him off the ball. It didn't matter where he was playing, though I suppose his best position was outside-left. He could go round you, or past you, or even straight through you sometimes!'

Bob Paisley on Billy Liddell

Albert Stubbins Is The One For Me

Record signing in 1946, and always
scoring – Albert Stubbins

You can keep Billy Liddell
You can keep Roger Hunt
David Johnson was a bit of a c*nt
You can keep Kenny Dalglish
You can keep Ian Rush
Albert Stubbins is the man for us

A-L-B-E-R-T
Albert Stubbins is the one for me

'My association with the Anfield Club has brought
me some of my finest memories of my career.'

Albert Stubbins

Liverpool We Love You

One of the original and most popular
songs still heard at matches today

We hate Nottingham Forest
We hate Evert*n too (they're sh*t)
We hate Man United
But Liverpool we love you

'My idea was to build Liverpool into a bastion of invincibility. Napoleon had that idea and he conquered the bloody world! And that's what I wanted. For Liverpool to be untouchable. My idea was to build Liverpool up and up and up until eventually everyone would have to submit and give in.'

Bill Shankly

Liverpool Bill (Liverpool Lou)

Another tribute to the great Bill Shankly

Anfield will always remember with pride
The Scot who commanded the Liverpool side
As sharp as a razor, his wit and his voice
His love of the game made him Liverpool's choice

O Liverpool Bill, you're our Liverpool Bill
Your name is a legend
Of courage and skill
You gave us the league
All the cups and the thrills
And that's why we love you
Our Liverpool Bill

Bill you will never be walking alone
The Kop will be with you away or at home
As long as we breathe we'll remember you still
O thank you forever, Our Liverpool Bill

A.E.HEATHCOTE

O Liverpool Bill, you're our Liverpool Bill
Your name is a legend
Of courage and skill
You gave us the league
All the cups and the thrills
And that's why we love you
Our Liverpool Bill

'I'm just one of the people who stands on the kop. They think the same as I do, and I think the same as they do. It's a kind of marriage of people who like each other.'

Bill Shankly on the fans

.

Liverpool Will Marmalise Milan
(Kelly The Boy from Killane)

Looking forward to the second leg of the 64/65 EC
Final which Liverpool eventually lost 4-3 on aggregate

What's the news, what's the news
O my brave Anfield fans
As you wait for the game to begin?
Milne and Byrne are both hurt
But each noble Red shirt
Will pray tonight that Liverpool win
Oh my boys they're the pride
Of the whole of Merseyside
They're the greatest of heroes to a man
So fling your favours aloft
And give three rousing cheers that
Liverpool will marmalise Milan

Tell me who is the giant
With the black curly hair
He who stands at the head of your band
Seven feet is his height
With some inches to spare
And he looks like a king in command
Ron Yeats is his name

The best skipper in the game
He's the greatest of heroes, what a man
So fling your favours aloft
And give three rousing cheers that
Liverpool will marmalise Milan

Now in three minutes flat
At the drop of a hat
Geoff Strong passed the ball to Callaghan
Well our wishes all came true
When young Roger went through
You should have heard the roar from the fans
Well boys they're the pride
Of the whole of Merseyside
They're the greatest of heroes to a man,
So fling your favours aloft
And give three rousing cheers that
Liverpool will marmalise Milan

'Liverpool without European football
is like a banquet without wine.'

Roy Evans

London Bridge Is Falling Down

Sung to any of the London clubs but originated
in the 65/66 season when Liverpool beat
Chelsea 2-1 at Anfield to seal a 7th title win

London Bridge is falling down
Falling down, falling down
London Bridge is falling down
Poor old Chelsea
Build it up with Red and white
Red and white, Red and white
Build it up with Red and white
Poor old Chelsea

'Where are you from?' 'I'm a Liverpool fan from London.' 'Well laddie, what's it like to be in heaven?'

Bill Shankly to a Liverpool fan

Billy The King

Yet more praise for Bill Shankly, as well as fullback
Gerry Byrne whom Shankly saved from the
transfer list when he arrived at Anfield

Oh lets drink, a drink, a drink
To Billy the king, the king, the king
The creator of the greatest team
For he invented professional football
And this year we'll win the league.

Now Gerry Byrne refused a tourniquet
When he's broken his collarbone
And they just rubbed on medicinal compound
And Gerry goes marching on

Oh lets drink, a drink, a drink
To Billy the king, the king, the king
The creator of the greatest team
For he invented professional football
And this year we'll win the league

'Liverpool was made for me and I was made for Liverpool.'

Bill Shankly

Big Ron Yeats

Praise for the big skipper

I'll tell you of our football team
And Liverpool is the name
We've won the cup, we've won the league
We're the finest in the game
We have the greatest skipper
Any manager could employ

Let's drink six crates
To big Ron Yeats
Bill Shankly's pride and joy
Yes drink six crates to big Ron Yeats
Bill Shankly's pride and joy

'I've just signed a colossus - come in and walk round him' … 'With him in defence we could play Arthur Askey in goal.'

Bill Shankly on Ron Yeats

The Greatest Team At Home
(The Green, Green Grass Of Home)

More praise for the club, the legends and the pitch

Well the old Kop looks the same
As I stand and watch the game
There's the green, green grass
That Liddell used to play on
Hunt, St.John and Thompson
Score the goals when Shankly wants them
It's good to watch the greatest team at home

Yes, we'll all go see Big Rowdy
Cheer the team that serves us proudly
It's good to watch the greatest team at home

'It's great grass at Anfield, professional grass!'

Bill Shankly comparing the Anfield
pitch to other grounds

The Billy Shankly Boys

A warning for the T*ffees

If you're tired and you're weary
And your heart skips a beat
You'll get your f*cking head kicked in
If you walk down Heyworth Street
If you come to The Albert
You'll hear our famous noise
Get out you Evert*n b*stards
We're the Billy Shankly boys

We're the boys from The Kop
We're loyal and we're true
And when we play the Evert*n
We're ready for a do
To the cry of 'No Surrender'
You'll hear our famous noise
Get out you Evert*n b*stards
We're the Billy Shankly boys

'If Evert*n were playing at the bottom of the garden,
I'd pull the curtains.'

Bill Shankly

When The Reds Go Marching In
(When The SaintsGo Marching In)

Although Southampton fans claim they were
the first to sing this version of Louis Armstrong's
classic, it has been a firm favourite amongst
the Reds for over forty years

Oh when the Reds (oh when the Reds)
Go marching in (go marching in)
Oh when the Reds go marching in
I want to be in that number
When the Reds go marching in
(Repeat as necessary)

'The trouble with referees is that they know the rules, but they don't know the game.'

Bill Shankly

Red And White Kop
(Yellow Submarine)

One of the most famous Liverpool songs, this has been heard at matches since the 'Beatlemania' of the 1960's

On a Saturday afternoon
We support a team called Liverpool
And we sing until we drop
In a Red and white Spion Kop

We all live in a Red and white Kop
A Red and white Kop
A Red and white Kop
We all live in a Red and white Kop
A Red and white Kop
A Red and white Kop

In a town where I was born
Lived a man who sailed the seas
And he told me of his pride
They were a famous football team
So we trailed to Anfield Road
Singing songs of victory
And there we found the holy ground
Of our hero Bill Shankly

We all live in Red and white Kop
A Red and white Kop
A Red and white Kop
We all live in a Red and white Kop
A Red and white Kop
A Red and white Kop

'At a football club, there's a holy trinity - the players, the manager and the supporters. Directors don't come into it. They are only there to sign the cheques.'

Bill Shankly on boardroom meetings

The Scarf My Father Wore
(The Sash My Father Wore)

Celebrating, amongst others, the first
FA Cup win which came in 1965

It was back in nineteen sixty five
On the very first day of May
Me Dad sang and danced for the lads in Red
As he walked down Wembley Way
Ian St. John scored the goal that won
The Cup we'd never won before
And as his son I love to wear
The scarf my father wore

It is old but it is beautiful
And its colours they are fine
It was worn in Paris, Wembley
In Rome and on the Rhine
My father wore it as a youth
In the bygone days of yore
And as his son I love to wear
The scarf my father wore

'We are the real people's club.'

Sammy Lee

Made For Shooting (These Boots Are Made For Walking)

Looking forward to the 1965-66 Cup Winners Cup
Round 2 match against Hungarian Army side Honved.
It ended 0-0 but the Reds went on to win 2-0 at Anfield

We'll all sing and raise our glasses up
When we win the European Cup
We've got the greatest side in the land
And we're known as Shankly's happy band
These boots are made for shooting
And that's just what they'll do
And when we get to Hungary they'll score a goal or two

They keep saying we'll do something new
And rest assured that's what we're gonna do
When Ian St John and Roger come inside
They'll give the Honved goalie such a fright
These boots are made for shooting
And that's just what they'll do
And when we get to Hungary they'll score a goal or two

Something else that really makes us sing
Is Callaghan and Thompson on the wing
Their centre forward may find things are cloudy
When he finds himself beneath big Rowdy
These boots are made for shooting
And that's just what they'll do
And when we get to Hungary they'll score a goal or two

'I don't believe everything Bill tells me about his players. Had they been that good, they'd not only have won the European Cup but the Ryder Cup, the Boat Race and even the Grand National!'

Celtic manager
Jock Stein on Bill Shankly

We'll Fight

Another warning to rival fans

We'll fight with no surrender
We'll fight for the boys in Red
We'll fight the fight for Liverpool
The team that Shankly led

We'll fight for Alun Evans
We'll fight for Ian St John
We'll fight the fight for Liverpool
The cream of Division One, two, three, four
Listen to the Kopites roar
Liverpool (clap, clap, clap)
Liverpool (clap, clap, clap)
Liverpool (clap, clap, clap)

'A lot of football success is in the mind. You must believe that you are the best and then make sure that you are. In my time at Liverpool we always said we had the best two teams in Merseyside, Liverpool and Liverpool reserves.'

Bill Shankly

Anfield Way

A song for cup finals played at Wembley, with special
remembrance for some of Liverpool's greatest players

Down Anfield Way the world is gay
All Kopites are to tingle
With rows and rows of crimson flags
From Bootle up to Dingle
The toast is to eleven men
Who wear the scarlet jersey
Their names will live forever more
Along the River Mersey

They'll take their place in history
Amongst the all time greats
Thompson, Byrne, St. John, and Hunt
And Skipper Rowdy Yeats
So let us sing a song or two
On Wembley's famous ground
And let London town re-echo
To that famous Mersey sound

They beat the Leeds two goals to one
And Rowdy met the queen
And Gerry broke his collar bone
As brave as you have seen
And when they bring that cup back home
Through streets all paved in Red
Those Liver Birds will fly away
Just like Bill Shankly said

'Take that bandage off. And what do you mean about YOUR knee? It's Liverpool's knee!'

Bill Shankly to Tommy Smith, who had a bandage on his injured knee

When Liverpool Win The Cup (When Johnny Comes Marching Home)

On the way to Liverpool's first ever FA Cup in 64/65

While on the bus from Villa Park hurrah, hurrah
I heard my mate make this remark hurrah, hurrah
We made poor Chelsea weep their fill
It's Liverpool two and Chelsea nil
And we'll all get drunk when Liverpool win the Cup

Here's to Lawrence, Milne, St John hurrah, hurrah
Byrne and Yeats and Stevenson hurrah, hurrah
Hunt and Thompson, what a man
Lawler, Smith and Callaghan
And we'll all get drunk when Liverpool win the Cup

From the Liverpool lads raise your glass hurrah, hurrah
To Stevenson who made the pass hurrah, hurrah
Thompson had them in a trance
Bonetti never stood a chance
And we'll all get drunk when Liverpool win the Cup

Here's to Lawrence, Milne, St John, hurrah, hurrah
Byrne and Yeats and Stevenson hurrah, hurrah
Hunt and Thompson what a man
Lawler, Smith and Callaghan
And we'll all get drunk when Liverpool win the Cup

It's Wembley on the 1st of May hurrah, hurrah
That's Leeds United's labour day hurrah, hurrah
We'll be there to cheer Bill Shankly's side
And bring the Cup to Merseyside
And we'll all get drunk when Liverpool win the Cup

Here's to Lawrence, Milne, St John hurrah, hurrah
Byrne and Yeats and Stevenson hurrah, hurrah
Hunt and Thompson what a man
Lawler, Smith and Callaghan
And we'll all get drunk when Liverpool win the Cup

And if it's a draw you'll hear us moan
Let's use the coin that beat Cologne
And we'll all get drunk when Liverpool win the Cup

'Yes Roger Hunt misses a few, but he gets
in the right place to miss them.'

Bill Shankly

Our Mighty Emlyn
(The Mighty Quinn)

Tribute to the late, great Emlyn 'Crazy Horse' Hughes

Come on without
Come on within
You've never seen nothing
Like our mighty Emlyn

'Liverpool are magic, Evert*n are tragic.'

Emlyn Hughes

The Sh*te In Royal Blue

Another one for Evert*n

We don't carry bottles
We don't carry lead
We only carry hatchets
To bury in your head
We are the supporters
Fanatics every one
We all hate Man City
And Leeds and Evert*n

We are the kings of Europe
The pride of Merseyside
We'll fight for no surrender
We'll fight for Shankly's pride
We hate Tottenham Hotspur
We hate Chelsea too
But most of all we hate the sh*te
Who play in Royal Blue

'The difference between Evert*n and the Queen Mary is that Evert*n carry more passengers!'

Bill Shankly

We Love You Liverpool

Although it is common to hear the chorus to this song sung by almost every club, this full version is unfortunately rare at games now

We love you Liverpool we do
We love you Liverpool we do
We love you Liverpool we do
Oh Liverpool we love you

Shankly is our hero
He showed us how to play
The mighty Reds of Europe
Are out to win today
He made a team of Champions
With every man a king
And every game we love to win
And this is what we sing

We love you Liverpool we do
We love you Liverpool we do
We love you Liverpool we do
Oh Liverpool we love you

A.E.HEATHCOTE

Clemence is our goalie
The best there is around
And Keegan is the greatest
That Shankly ever found
Heighway is our favourite
A wizard of the game
And here's the mighty Toshack
To do it once again

We love you Liverpool we do
We love you Liverpool we do
We love you Liverpool we do
Oh Liverpool we love you

We've won the League
We've won the Cup
We're masters of the game
And just to prove how good we are
We'll do it all again
We've got another team to beat
And so we've got to try
'Cos we're the best in all the land
And that's the reason why
We love you Liverpool we do
We love you Liverpool we do
We love you Liverpool we do
Oh Liverpool we love you

'Mind you, I've been here during the bad times too -
one year we came second.'

Bob Paisley

A Little Touch Of Scotland

Respect for the great man

A little touch of Scotland came to Liverpool one day
He looked around and said 'Och man aye, this is where
I'll stay'
And from that moment he worked hard to build a team
so grand
And now today we have the greatest team in all the land

Shankly, oh yes Bill Shankly
Shankly we love you
For all the things you've done for us
While here at Liverpool
Bill Shanky we thank you

Nowhere would you find a man who is the same as he
And all who meet him love him for his humility
For that and many other things our thanks we give to him
And do you see we're talking of Bill Shankly, aye that's him

Shankly, oh yes Bill Shankly
Shankly we love you
For all the things you've done for us
While here at Liverpool
Bill Shankly we thank you

'If Shankly had been paid overtime,
he'd have been a millionaire.'

Tommy Docherty on Bill Shankly

A Long Way To Wembley Stadium
(A Long Way To Tipperary)

But we don't mind…

It's a long way to Wembley Stadium
It's a long way to go

It's a long way to Wembley Stadium
To see the greatest team I know

So it's goodbye Upper Parly
Farewell Clayton Square

It's a long, long way to Wembley Stadium
But Liverpool will be there

'The goal looked as big as the Mersey Tunnel.'

Ian St John after his winning goal in
the 1965 FA Cup Final against Leeds

Every Other Saturday

A brief history of just some of Liverpool's achievements

Every other Saturday's me half day off
And it's off to the match I go
I like to take a stroll along the Anfield Road
Me and me old pal Joe
I like to see the lasses with their Red scarves on
I like to hear the Kopites roar
But I don't have to tell that best of all
Is when we see Liverpool score

We've won the English League about a thousand times
And UEFA was a simple do
We've played some exhibitions in the FA Cup
We are the Wembley Wizards too
But when we won the European Cup in Rome
Like we should have done years before
We gathered down at Anfield
Boys a hundred thousand strong
To give the boys a welcome home

Kenny, oh, Kenny
I'd walk a million miles for one of your goals
Oh Kenny, oh Kenny

'I owe Bob more than I owe anybody else in the game. There will never be another like him.'

Kenny Dalglish on Bob Paisley

We're The Champions

And the most successful team in British history

Here in Liverpool we all say with pride
We are the supporters of the greatest football side
We are the Champions, yes we are the kings
We are the Champions and that is why we sing

Liverpool are the team
We're the best you've ever seen
You can stick United and the rest
Liverpool are still the best
Na, na, na, na, na, na,
Hey, hey, we're the Champions

We have played the best in Europe and at home
And our sportsmanship and skill to all is known
We are the Champions, there can be no doubt
We are the Champions and that is why we shout

Liverpool are the team
We're the best you've ever seen
You can stick United and the rest
Liverpool are still the best
Na, na, na, na, na, na,
Hey, hey, we're the Champions

We thank all those teams that gave us such a fright
Now as your Champions we'll set the world alight
We are the Champions, shout it from the Kop
We are the Champions, that Liverpool are top

Liverpool are the team
We're the best you've ever seen
You can stick United and the rest
Liverpool are still the best
Na, na, na, na, na, na,
Hey, hey, we're the Champions

'Liverpool wouldn't be the club it is today without Bill Shankly and Bob Paisley and the players who played there. When I first went there it was a typical Second Division ground and look at it now!'

Ian Callaghan

Where Are The Lads?
(The Boys Of The Old Brigade)

Nostalgic homage to the Liverpool fans
who watched their team lose
To Inter Milan in 64/65 and beat Etienne in 76/77

Oh father why are you so sad
Your face so pale and fraught
When all us Reds are proud and glad
Of the team that we support
Oh son I see in memory's view
Days of long ago you see
When we cheered and sang
And from the Kop there rang
Songs of Liverpool F.C

Where are the lads who stood with me
At Milan and Etienne?
Oh it grieves me that I will never see
The Spion Kop again

From Cantril Farm the call to arms
Was heard by one and all
And from Garston came brave young men
To answer Shankly's call

I think of them at St Etienne
Who made the rafters shake
And in 65, they brought the Kop alive
And made poor Inter quake

Where are the lads who stood with me
At Milan and Etienne?
Oh it grieves me that I will never see
The Spion Kop again

And so my son I've told you why
On this dark day I sigh
As I recall great players all
From the glory days gone by
Who played before the greatest fans
Their singing never stopped
Oh they sang and cheered and Liverpool revered
On the mighty Spion Kop

Where are the lads who stood with me
At Milan and Etienne?
Oh it grieves me that I will never see
The Spion Kop again

'If Shankly was the Anfield foreman, Paisley was the brickie, ready to build an empire with his own hands.'

Tommy Smith

A Packet Of Crisps

A song for the T*ffee's of the Gladwys Street terrace

You get more noise from a packet of crisps
Than you do from the Gladwys Street

You get more noise from a packet of crisps
Than you do from the Gladwys Street

You get silence here quiet there
Not a sound from anywhere

You get more noise from a packet of crisps
Than you do from the Gladwys Street

'On awaiting Evert*n's arrival for a derby game at Anfield, **Bill Shankly** gave a box of toilet rolls to the doorman and said: 'Give them these when they arrive – they'll need them!'

The Fields Of Anfield Road
(The Fields Of Athenry)

Based on the 'Fields of Athenry' this song was first sung
by Celtic fans and later adopted by the Anfield faithful

Outside the Shankly Gates
I heard a Kopite calling
Shankly they have taken you away
But you left a great eleven
Before you went to heaven
Now it's glory round the Fields of Anfield Road

All round the Fields of Anfield Road
Where once we watched the King Kenny play
(and he could play)
We had Heighway on the wing
We had dreams and songs to sing
Of the glory round the Fields of Anfield Road

Outside the Paisley Gates
I heard a Kopite calling
Paisley they have taken you away
You led the great 11
Back in Rome in 77

And the Redmen they are still playing the same way
All round the Fields of Anfield Road
Where once we watched the King Kenny play
(and he could play)
We had Heighway on the wing
We had dreams and songs to sing
Of the glory round the Fields of Anfield Road

'I just hoped that after the trials and tribulations of my early years in management, someone up high would smile on me and guide my hand. My plea was answered when we got Kenny Dalglish. What a player, what a great professional!'

Bob Paisley

Those Were The Days

A classic terrace chant sung for many years
and made famous in the days when rival
fans would attack each other inside the ground

Those were the days my friends
We took the Stretford End
We took the Shed
The North Bank, Highbury
We took the Geordies too
We fought for Liverpool
We are the Kop
Of Liverpool F.C

'If you can't make decisions in life, you're a bloody menace. You'd be better becoming an MP!'

Bill Shankly

The Men From The Spion Kop
(The Shores Of Tripoli)

.More support for the team

We are the men from Anfield's Spion Kop
Our team is Liverpool F.C
We like to sing and shout
Because we know
We'll cheer the team to victory
For it's a great team you'll agree
And we'll go down in history
We've won the cup, been Champions too
And today we'll murder you
We're the Liverpool FC
And if you go to any ground
You'll always hear our songs
To see our team we'll be there
For we know our team will
Fight, fight, fight
It's gonna be a glorious
Sight, sight, sight
We all agree it's going to be
Another glorious victory
For the Liverpool F.C

'The only thing I fear is missing an open goal in front of the Kop. I would die if that were to happen. When they start singing 'You'll Never Walk Alone' my eyes start to water. There have been times when I've actually been crying while I've been playing.'

Kevin Keegan

Poor Scouser Tommy
(Red River Valley And The Sash)

Sung by Liverpool fans for many years this is actually
a combination of two songs; Red River Valley and
The Sash and is one of the most popular songs still
sung by the Reds

Let me tell you the story of a poor boy
Who was sent far away from his home
To fight for his king and his country
And also the old folks back home

So they put him in a Highland division
Sent him off to a far foreign land
Where the flies swarm around in their thousands
And there's nothing to see but the sands

In a battle that started next morning
Under an Arabian sun
I remember that poor Scouser Tommy
Who was shot by an old Nazi gun

As he lay on the battle field dying, dying, dying
With the blood gushing out of his head (of his head)
As he lay on the battle field dying, dying, dying
These were the last words he said...

Oh... I am a Liverpudlian
I come from the Spion Kop
I like to sing, I like to shout
I go there quite a lot (every week)

We support the team that's dressed in Red
A team that we all know
A team that we call Liverpool
And to glory we will go

We've won the League, we've won the Cup
We've been to Europe too
We played the T*ffees for a laugh
And we left them feeling blue - Five Nil

One two
One two three
One two three four
Five nil

Rush scored one
Rush scored two
Rush scored three
And Rush scored four

'He's better than Brian Lara because he's
600 not out. What a guy.'

Roy Evans on Ian Rush's
600th appearance for Liverpool

Johnny Barnes

Praise for legendary winger John Barness

Oh his father was a soldier (oh his father was a soldier)
He couldn't play the football (he couldn't play the football)
His son he played for Watford (his son he played for Watford)
But now he plays for Liverpool
(but now he plays for Liverpool)

His name is Johnny Barnes (his name is Johnny Barnes)
He comes from Jamaica (he comes from Jamaica)
And if you read the papers (and if you read the papers)
He's going to Italia (he's going to Italia)

Oh, no, no
No, no, no
No, no, no
No, no, no

'Barnes did what we expected him to do. He made a goal, scored one, and entertained. You remember that.'

Kenny Dalglish after John Barnes Anfield debut for Liverpool in a 2-0 win over Oxford in 1987

Johnny on the Ball

More praise for John Barnes

We love John Barnes
We love John Barnes
We love John Barnes
Johnny on the ball

He's fantastic
Legs elastic
He stands proud while all defenders fall

Shout it loud like
Shout it all around like
Shout it in the ground like
Or anywhere at all, that

We love John Barnes
We love John Barnes
We love John Barnes
Johnny on the ball

'They compare Steve McManaman to Steve Heighway and he's nothing like him, but I can see why - it's because he's a bit different.'

Kevin Keegan

I'm Forever Blowing Bubbles

A play on words for the classic West Ham song,
though other London clubs don't go unmentioned

I'm forever blowing bubbles
Pretty bubbles in the air
They fly so high
They reach the sky
And like West Ham they fade and die

Tottenham's always running
Chelsea's running too
And when you come to Anfield
We'll be running after you

Liverpool (clap, clap, clap)
Liverpool (clap, clap, clap)
Liverpool (clap, clap, clap)

'If you're in the penalty area and don't know what to do with the ball, put it in the net and we'll discuss the options later.'

Bob Paisley

With A Shotgun On My Knee (Oh Susanna)

A song from the darker days of football as well
as a bit of competition between the Kop
and the Anfield Road End

Oh I went up to Old Trafford with a shotgun on my knee
And I went down to the scoreboard with the men from L.F.C
Oh my darling, don't you cry for me
'Cos I'm going to Man United with the boys of L.F.C

Oh I went to Tottenham Hotspur with a shotgun on my knee
We took all the Tottenham then the North Bank Highbury
Oh and the Chelsea we took your f*cking Shed
At Fulham Broadway station all the blue tw*ts they were dead

Oh I'm going to Man United with a shotgun on my knee
We're gonna take the scoreboard we're the boys of L.F.C
We are the Road End the pride of Merseyside
We do all the fighting while the Kopites run and hide

Oh I went to Man United with a shotgun on my knee
We went to take the scoreboard for the famous L.F.C
We are the Kopites, we all went to Rome
We all went to West Ham while the Road End stayed at home

'Shanks was the father figure but Roger Hunt was something special. It might sound daft but just picking up his sweaty kit gave me satisfaction.'

Phil Thompson

A Scouser In Gay Paris

Looking forward to the 1981 European Cup Final

How would you like to be
A Scouser in Gay Paris
Walking along on the banks of the Seine
Winning the European Cup once again
We'll go up the Eiffel Tower
And stay up there half an hour
'Cos we won't be too late
When we celebrate
We're the Scousers in Gay Paris
We'll visit the Follies Bergere
They like to see Scousers there
The women are lovely
With skin like a peach
But they'll never move it like Kenny Dalglish
How would you like to be
A Scouser in Gay Paris

'He's better than Platini, certainly better than Rumminegge and Maradona. For me he is the greatest footballer in the world.'

Graeme Souness on Kenny Dalglish

O Come All Ye Faithful

An invitation for others to come and see
what a successful team really looks like

O come all ye faithful
Joyful and triumphant
O come ye, O come ye to Anfield

Come and behold them
They're the Kings of Europe
O come let us adore them
O come let us adore them
O come let us adore them
Liiiiiverpool

'If a player is not interfering with play or seeking to gain an advantage, then he should be.'

Bill Shankly

The Best Behaved Supporters (She'll Be Coming Round The Mountain)

Liverpool fans telling it like it is

We're the best behaved supporters in the land (when we win)
We're the best behaved supporters in the land (when we win)
We're the best behaved supporters
The best behaved supporters
We're the best behaved supporters in he land (when we win)

We're a right shower of b*stards when we lose (when we lose)
We're a right shower of b*stards when we lose (when we lose)
We're a right shower of b*stards
A right shower of b*stards
We're a right shower of b*stards when we lose (but we don't)

'Just go out and drop a few hand grenades all over the place son.'

Bill Shankly to
Kevin Keegan

Wash Your Mouth Out Son
(Que Sera)

A song that can be (and often is) changed
for most rival clubs but which still has a
special place for 'us' and 'them'

When I was just a little boy
I asked my mother what shall I be?
Shall I be Reds?
Shall I be T*ffees?
Here's what she said to me
Wash your mouth out son
And fetch your father's gun
And shoot the T*ffee scum
Reds are number one
Liverpool (clap, clap, clap)
Liverpool (clap, clap, clap)
Liverpool (clap, clap, clap)

'It's best being a striker. If you miss five then score the winner, you're a hero. The goalkeeper can play a blinder, then let one in... and he's a villain.'

Ian Rush

Oh Billy Bingham
(My Old Man's A Dustman)

A song for T*ffee's Billy Bingham and Bob Latchford

Oh Billy Bingham
He won the Evert*n Tote
And with the money that he won
He bought himself a goat
The Goat his name was Latchford
He couldn't score a goal
And as for Billy Bingham
You can stick him up your hole

'Don't worry Alan. At least you'll be
able to play close to a great team!'

Bill Shankly to Alan Ball
who just signed for Evert*n

Underneath The Floodlights
(Lili Marlene)

The original song has been around for nearly
100 years and was a big favourite during both
World Wars before it was adopted by the Kop

Underneath the floodlights
Down in Dusseldorf
All the Kop were singing
Bevvied up of course
We've been to Lisbon and to Rome
And our team never walk alone
We're going off to Europe to bring the Cup back home

All the way from Anfield to the gates of Rome
All the way from Anfield to bring the trophy home
Nothing can stop us come what may
We'll have our say, this is our day
Liverpool's Red army
Is marching on it's way

'Sometimes I feel I'm hardly wanted in this Liverpool team. If I get two or three saves to make, I've had a busy day.'

Ray Clemence

The Pride Of Merseyside
(Una Paloma Blanca)

Sung prior to both the 76/77 and 83/84 EC Finals

When the ground is full of Kopites
And the kick off time is near
Here's the song we'll be singing
When the boys in Red appear
Liverpool are the greatest
The greatest team in the land
Liverpool have the greatest
The greatest fans in the land
We are the pride
Of Merseyside

Liverpool they are pure magic
And no matter where they play
When we go all over Europe
You can hear the people say
Liverpool are the greatest
The greatest team in the land
Liverpool have the greatest
The greatest fans in the land
We are the pride
Of Merseyside

We'll collect another trophy
When we go and play in Rome
And all the Kopites will be singing
When we're on our way back home
Liverpool are the greatest
The greatest team in the land
Liverpool have the greatest
The greatest fans in the land
We are the pride
Of Merseyside

'Chairman Mao has never seen a
greater show of Red strength.'

Bill Shankly

The Blue-nose B*stards

More abuse for the T*ffees

The Blue-nose b*stards aren't the Champions anymore
They went to Nottingham Forest and only got a draw
Then they went to Oxford and they couldn't even score
The Blue-nose b*stards aren't the Champions anymore

'Sickness would not have kept me away from this one. If I'd been dead, I would have had them bring the casket to the ground, prop it up in the stands and cut a hole in the lid.'

Bill Shankly after beating
Evert*n in the 1971 FA cup semi-final

Oh Goodison Park Is A Terrible Place

A Song for Evert*n

Oh Goodison Park is a terrible place
Some people say it's a f*cking disgrace
With half backs and full backs and centre backs too
Their hands in their pockets
With f*ck all to do

Now the Street End they scream and the Park End they shout
For fourteen long years they've had f*ck all to mouth
Some people say it's the scourge of our town
The rest of us say burn the f*cking place down

'I know this is a sad occasion but I think that Dixie would be amazed to know that even in death he could draw a bigger crowd than Evert*n can on a Saturday afternoon.'

Bill Shankly at Dixie Dean's funeral

A Liverbird Upon My Chest
(Ballad Of The Green Berets)

Recalling past glories, this song is constantly added to as
the years pass but this remains the most popular version

Here's a song about a football team
The greatest team you've ever seen
A team that play total football
They've won the league, Europe and all

A Liverbird upon my chest
We are the men, of Shankly's best
A team that plays the Liverpool way
And wins the Championship in May

With Kenny Dalglish on the ball
He was the greatest of them all
And Ian Rush, four goals or two
Left Evert*nians feeling blue

A Liverbird upon my chest
We are the men, of Shankly's best
A team that plays the Liverpool way
And wins the Championship in May

Now if you go down Goodison Way
Hard luck stories you hear each day
There's not a trophy to be seen
'Cos Liverpool have swept them clean

A Liverbird upon my chest
We are the men, of Shankly's best
A team that plays the Liverpool way
And wins the Championship in May

Now on the glorious 10th of May
There's laughing Reds on Wembley Way
We're full of smiles and joy and glee
It's Evert*n 1 and Liverpool 3

A Liverbird upon my chest
We are the men, of Shankly's best
A team that plays the Liverpool way
And wins the Championship in May

Now on the 20th of May
We're laughing still on Wembley Way
Those Evert*nians are feeling blue
It's Liverpool 3 and Evert*n 2

A Liverbird upon my chest
We are the men, of Shankly's best
A team that plays the Liverpool way
And wins the Championship in May

And as we sang round Goodison Park
With crying blues all in a nark
They're probably crying still
At Liverpool 5 and Evert*n nil.

A Liverbird upon my chest
We are the men, of Shankly's best
A team that plays the Liverpool way
And wins the Championship in May

We remember them with pride
Those mighty Reds of Shankly's side
And Kenny's boys of '88
There's never been a side so great

A Liverbird upon my chest
We are the men, of Shankly's best
A team that plays the Liverpool way
And wins the Championship in May

Now back in 1965
When great Bill Shankly was alive
We're playing Leeds, the score's 1-1
When it fell to the head of Ian St John

A Liverbird upon my chest
We are the men, of Shankly's best
A team that plays the Liverpool way
And wins the Championship in May

On April 15th '89
What should have been a joyous time
Ninety six Friends, we all shall miss
And all the Kopites want justice (JUSTICE)

'The word fanatic has been used many times. I think it's more than fanaticism. It's a religion to them. The thousands who come here, come to worship. It's a sort of shrine, it isn't a football ground.'

Bill Shankly on the fans

The Twelve Days of Christmas

A celebration of a great side

On the 12th day of Christmas my true love gave to me ...
12 David Hodgson
11 Graeme Souness
10 Craig Johnstone
9 Ian Rush
8 Sammy Lee
7 Kenny Dalglish
6 Alan Hansen
5 Ronnie Whelan
4 Mark Lawrenson
3 Alan Kennedy
2 Philip Neal
And Brucie in our goal

'I was Bob's first signing. He changed my life, as he did so many others. He gave us great memories and you can't put a price on that. He made me an adopted Scouser.'

Phil Neal

Hark Now Hear The Scousers Sing (Hark The Herald Angels)

A song for anytime Liverpool play Evert*n

Hark now hear
The Scousers sing
The T*ffees ran away
And we will fight for ever more
Because of derby day

Hark now hear
The Scousers sing
We won again today
We'll always fight
The Blue-nosed s*ite
When it comes to derby day

'I told this player. Listen son, you haven't broken your leg. It's all in your mind!'

Bill Shankly

The Wings Of A Sparrow
(Bring My Bonnie Back To Me)

A song that also works well for most
favourite teams. T*ffee's fits nicely too

If I had the wings of a sparrow
If I had the a*se of a crow
I'd fly over Man U tomorrow
And sh*t on the b*stards below (below)
I'd sh*t on the b*stards below
Sh*t on, Sh*t on, Sh*t on the b*stards below (below)
I'd sh*t on the b*stards below

'Me having no education. I had to use my brains.'

Bill Shankly

The Famous Man Utd
(The Battle Hymn Of The Republic)

Just to let them know who the real
Kings of Europe are...

The famous Man Utd went to Rome to see the Pope
The famous Man Utd went to Rome to see the Pope
The famous Man Utd went to Rome to see the Pope
And this is what he said ...
Who the f*ck are Man Utd?
Who the f*ck are Man Utd?
Who the f*ck are Man Utd?
And the Reds go marching on, on, on

'I don't like champagne, I don't smoke cigars, I haven't any real jewellery at all, apart from the 8 pieces of gold I picked up at Anfield. The most important relationship at a football club is not between the manager and the chairman, but the players and the fans'

John Toshack

Bjornebye In My Gang
(I'm The Leader Of The Gang)

With a name like that, how could anyone resist ? . .

You'll never believe it
Come on, come on
You'll never believe it
Come on, come on
You'll never believe it
Come on, come on

Bjornebye in my gang, my gang, my gang
Bjornebye in my gang
Oh yeah

He's our left back
He's our left back
It's Stig Inge at the back oh yeah

'All players are born. Anyone who tells you that they can make players are very stupid people.'

Bill Shankly

Vegard Heggem
(Good King Wenceslas)

Tribute to the Norwegian right back after he
scored in a 3-1 Boxing
Day win over Middlesbrough in the 98/99 season

Vegard Heggem scored a goal
On the feast of Stephen
Vegard Heggem scored a goal
As the fans were leaving
Liverpool they won three one
Carragher and Jamie
Vegard Heggem scored a goal
All the fans went crazy

'I was like any other Liverpool fan, in awe of the team and in awe of Bill Shankly. Everyone knew that Shankly was creating a monster; this was no ordinary football team.'

Phil Thompson

Side By Side

Looking forward to the success of the managerial part-
nership between Gerard Houllier and Phil Thompson

We've no longer got Shankly or Paisley
Or a horse that is gangly and crazy
But we've Thommo and Ged
Wearing the Red
Side by side

We've all left the 90's behind us
But in Europe you can still find us
With Thommo and Ged
Wearing the Red
Side by side

They'll go and they'll win all the trophies
So the rest of the world they can see
That it's Thommo and Ged
Wearing the Red
Side by side

So we've all left the 90's behind us
But in Europe you can still find us
With Thommo and Ged
Wearing the Red
Side by side

'I used to stand on the Kop when I was here in 1969. The atmosphere and passion on the pitch as well as the terraces was intoxicating and Liverpool became part of me from that day on.'

Gerard Houllier

Robbie Fowler (Amore)

Homage to the great striker

When the ball hits the net
It's a fairly safe bet that it's Fowler
Robbie Fowler

And When Liverpool score
You will hear the Kop roar 'oh it's Fowler'
Robbie Fowler

Ian Rush, Roger Hunt
Who's the best man up front? 'Oh it's Fowler'
Robbie Fowler

He's the King of the Kop
He's the best of the lot
Robbie Fowler
Robbie Fowler

'Ever since I started at Liverpool as a kid the fans have taken to me and any player will tell you when the supporters of your club are behind you then that helps an awful lot. I just can't thank them enough. They've given me so much support over the years and I'm grateful for that.'

Robbie Fowler

Reds Never Tire (Mull Of Kintyre)

Another song about the good old days

Far have I traveled and much have I seen
The years spent in Europe now number twenty
While all those around us they fade and they tire
You'll hear the Kop singing
'The Reds never tire'

The Reds never tire, you'll hear the Kop singing
You'll play with the fire, that just keeps us winning
The Reds never tire

Now Evert*n are finished and Leeds they are dead
Benfica and Gladbach their faces are Red
The cockneys are bottom they won't get much higher
But youll hear the Kop singing
'The Reds never tire'

The Reds never tire, you'll hear the Kop singing
You'll play with the fire, that just keeps us winning
The Reds never tire

Now back in the sixties were Hunt and St John
With Stevo and Rowdie but sadly they're gone
Today we've got Michael and Robbie on fire
And you'll hear the Kop singing
'The Reds never tire'

The Reds never tire, you'll hear the Kop singing
You'll play with the fire, that just keeps us winning
The Reds never tire

'Shankly had us believing we were the fittest team in the league. He would tell the press, 'My boys are training hard', when he'd given us the day off. We'd read the next day how we'd been running around like madmen when we'd been to the baths and had a massage.'

Ian St John

Men Of Anfield (Men Of Harlech)

Tribute to some of the greats

Stevie Heighway's always running
John Toshack's always scoring
Then you'll hear the Kopites roaring
Toshack is our king

Men of Anfield here's our story
We have gone from great to glory
We're the greatest team in Europe
Dalglish is our king

Paddy Berger's always running
Michael Owen's always scoring
Then you hear the Kopites roaring
Fowler is our king

'Roy Evans said to me, 'Karl, I have a new young talent that I want you to see.' And then, of course, I saw Michael playing in training, and I said to myself, 'This boy is not just a young talent, he is going to be a bloody great player!'

Karl-Heinz Riedle

Gary Macca (Alouette)

Tribute to Gary McAllister

Gary Macca, Gary, Gary Macca
Gary Macca, Gary, Gary Mac
Oh we love your baldy head
(oh we love your baldy head)
Your baldy head (your baldy head)
You're Gary Mac (You're Gary Mac)
Gary Macca, Gary, Gary Macca

Gary Macca, Gary, Gary Mac
Oh we loved your derby goal
(oh we loved your derby goal)

Oh we loved your Barca Pen
(oh we loved your Barca pen)

Oh we loved your Spurs Peno
(oh we loved your Spurs peno)

Oh we loved your Coventry goal
(oh we loved your Coventry goal)

Oh we loved your Bradford goal
(Oh we loved your Bradford goal)

Oh we loved your Dortmund Pen
(Oh we loved your Dortmund pen)

Oh we love your sweet right foot
(Oh we love your sweet right foot)

Oh we got you on a free
(Oh we got you on a free)

Oh we went and won all three
(Oh we went and won all three)

Oh Gary Macca, Gary, Gary Macca
Gary Macca, Gary, Gary Mac

'I will never forget today and I want to thank all the fans who gave me such a great ovation. They were immense. I thought I would get a decent reception but that surpassed all my wildest dreams. That sort of ovation is normally reserved for players who have won European Cups for a club. It was a brilliant day and it was nice to hear the Kop's humour at its best again when they were telling me to go back to Coventry.'

Gary McAllister after his last game for Liverpool at Anfield

Gary Mac the Knife (Mack the Knife)

More praise for Gary McAllister

Easter Monday at the sh*t pit
Blue scum crying what a sight
Walking wounded, gaping gashes
Left by Gary Mac the knife

Twisted faces spitting venom
Season tickets torn to shreds
Smashed up bus stops, housewives beaten
As Reds lay w*nking in their beds

Round to my house all the boys came
We won't go there any more
Woke the kids up doing the conga
At half past f*cking four

Two were hanging from the lampshade
Another clung to the curtain pole
I got my head stuck in the ceiling
When Gary scored that f*cking goal
Oh what a party, what a scoreline
I've never been so bloody pissed
Andrew Lloyd Webber or Walt Disney
Couldn't have written a better script

Crying bastards, sobbing a*seholes
Wondering why all round the ground
You disrespected the minutes silence
So what goes around comes around

You are the pimple on our a*seholes
You're the sh*te between our toes
You're the skidmarks in our undies
And the bogies up our nose

I'm so happy I'm doing strange things
Last night I even kissed the wife
Said 'excuse me' when I farted
Because of Gary Mac the knife

'Playing at Anfield is special and it is a shame I couldn't play there earlier in my career, because there were rumours at one point that they were interested, but it never happened. But you don't turn down Liverpool when they come calling and I finally made it there in what was a fantastic part of my career.'

Gary McAllister

Henchoz (Hi Ho)

A tribute to the Swiss centre half

Henchoz, Henchoz
Henchoz, Henchoz, Henchoz
When they attack he's always back
Henchoz
Henchoz, Henchoz, Henchoz

'Liverpool players must play like a lion, give his all. There must be determination, commitment and resolve to be a Liverpool player.'

Gerard Houllier

The Face on Michael Ball
(The Animals Went In Two By Two)

A song regarding Liverpool's 3-2 win
over Evert*n when Gary
McAllister scored a free kick from range

Look at the face on Michael Ball hurrah, hurrah
Look at the face on Michael Ball hurrah, hurrah
Look at the face on Michael Ball
McCallister bent it round the wall
And we all went to town when Liverpool beat the Blues

'It has to be the one against Evert*n.'

Gary McAllister on his
favourite goal for Liverpool

One Nil Down... (This Old Man)

A reference to Michael Owen's late brace against
Arsenal to win the 00/01 FA Cup Final

One nil down
Two one up
Michael Owen won the Cup
When a top class Paddy pass
Gave the lad the ball
Poor old Arsenal won f*ck all

'We don't have any splits here. The players country is Liverpool Football Club and their language is football.'

Gerard Houllier when
questioned on squad rotation

We're Going To Cardiff Twice/ We're Going To Italy (Que Sera)

Sung in the 00/ 01 season after winning the League
Cup and heading to the Millenium Stadium again
for the FA Cup Final. The variation was first heard
in 1977, when Liverpool were on their way
to winning the EC in Rome

Tell me ma, me ma
To put the Champagne on ice
We're going to Cardiff twice
Tell me ma, me ma

Tell me ma, me ma
I don't want no tea, no tea
We're going to Italy
Tell me ma, me ma

'Playing Roma in Rome in the European Cup final and scoring a penalty in the shoot out to help us win it. That was my very last kick for Liverpool and it doesn't really get any better than that.'

Graeme Souness

A Kopite Wonderland
(Walking In A Winter Wonderland)

A celebration of Liverpool's 3-0 win over
Evert*n at Goodison in the 03/04 season

Owen runs and then he hits it
Owen runs and then he chips it
What a beautiful way
To score ten in a day
Walking in a Kopite wonderland

Rooney runs and then he hoofs it
Rooney runs and then he spoofs it
What a beautiful way
To miss ten in a day
Walking in a Kopite wonderland

'He's the most exciting thing to happen to English soccer in years. Rarely have I seen someone accomplish so much in so little time.'

Roy Evans on Michael Owen

Hey Big Didi (Hey Big Spender)

Homage to midfielder Dietmar 'Didi' Hamann

The minute you walked in the joint Didi
I could see you were Hamann of distinction
A real big player
Good passing, so refined
You could always play in any midfield of mine
So let me get right to the point Didi
I don't pop my cork for every player I see
Hey big Didi, (hey big Didi)
Score another goal for me
Da, da, da, da, da, da

'Fear.'

Dietmar Hamann when asked what
emotions Germans felt towards Michael Owen

Bootle Boy

Sung to the centre back after he 'returned' a coin that
was thrown at him by an Arsenal fan

Bootle boy
Born and bred
Jamie Carragher is a Red
Bootle boy
Born and bred
He throws coins at cockney's heads

'I want to stay here for the rest of my career. I'm not interested in this new FIFA rule where players can buy themselves out of their contracts. I know it's there but I don't know anything about it because it's something I wouldn't do. .. My ambition is to wear that Red shirt as long as I can and I'd be absolutely gutted if I ever had to leave.'

Jamie Carragher

The Liverbird Of Liverpool F.C
(Yellow Rose Of Texas)

A song for the famous Liverpool crest

Have you ever heard of the Liverbird of Liverpool F.C?
Proud on the chest of the team that's best
The team for you and me
The team of Billy Liddell, Dalglish and Bill Shankly
We'll fight, fight, fight
For the Red and white of Liverpool F.C

'You may have found me mean and thirsty in my search for trophies, but the bad news is the man who is taking my place is hungrier than me. Fagan's the name and I don't think he'll need any help from the Artful Dodger!'

Bob Paisley on Joe Fagan

Carra's Dad (Quartermasters Stores)

In reference to Jamie Carragher's dad being
banned from football stadia after being arrested
for being drunk at a football match

He's Red
He's sound
He's banned from every ground
Carra's dad, Carra's dad

He's Red
He's great
He can't get past the gate
Carra's dad, Carra's dad

'Who's bigger than Liverpool?'

Jamie Carragher when asked if
he'd thought of moving to a bigger club

Scouse And Sound

Another reference to Jamie Carragher's
coin 'throwing' antics

He's Scouse
He's sound
He'll tw*t you with a pound
Carragher, Carragher

'Along with John Terry, Carragher is the best defender in the country. His reading of the game is second to none and he has got such a wonderful football mind. Quite simply, Jamie epitomizes everything that is good about Liverpool FC, past and present'

John Aldridge on Jamie Carragher

Blame It On Traore
(Blame It On The Boogie)

Sung after Djimi Traore's spectacular own
goal in the 04/05 FA Cup defeat to Burnley

Don't blame it on the Hamman
Don't blame it on the Biscan
Don't blame it on the Finnan
Blame it on Traore

He just can't
He just can't
He just can't control his feet

He just can't
He just can't
He just can't control his feet

'We've got a great team spirit - It doesn't matter how many goals we go down, we'll keep fighting till the end.'

Steven Gerrard

Our Fullbacks (This Old Man)

Praise for Finnan. Not quite for Traore

We've got a right back called Steve Finnan
When he plays we're always winning 'em
He plays the ball outside and in again
We've got a right back called Steve Finnan

We had a left back called Traore
When he played it was a different story
The goal at Burnley was his glory
We had a left back called Traore

'He's definitely heading towards that legendary status if he carries on the way he has done for the last few years'

Phil Neal on Steve Finnan

The Kop Is In No Doubt
(The Hokey Cokey)

Sung following Luis Garcia's controversial goal that
put Chelsea out of the CL Semi Final 1-0 in 2005

Did that ball go in?
Did that ball stay out?
In, out, in, out
The Kop is in no doubt
When Luis Garcia comes and scores a goal
That's what he's all about
Oh Jose, Jose, Jose
Oh Jose, Jose, Jose
Oh Jose, Jose, Jose
He knocked your Chelsea out

'We found out we had drawn them in the knockout round after training, and you should have seen the faces of Steven Gerrard and Jamie Carragher – it was an immense 'bring them on' look. I don't think Barcelona realise what Anfield in the second leg can do to them.'

Luis Garcia speaking about the
upcoming C.L. matches against Barcelona

Rafa In Istanbul

A response to Chelsea following their defeat
to Liverpool in the CL semi final and their
subsequent failure to buy Steven Gerrard

Mourinho said 'don't worry
Chelsea have nothing to fear'
But how he went so quiet
When up popped Luis Garcia
His shot it had no power
But the lino he said
'That's a goal'
And now he's taking Rafa
On the road to Istanbul
Rafael, Rafael, Rafa in Istanbul

Benitez said 'don't worry
I'll wipe away your tears'
'Cos Stevie G's a Red
And a Red he'll be for years
We don't want your John Terry
Stick your Lampard up you're a*se
'Cos Carra' is here
And Gerrard's a Red
And they're both staying ours
Rafael, Rafael, Rafa in Istanbul

'I can say to him in the next ten years we will compare trophies at Chelsea and at Liverpool. And he will lose.'

Jose Mourinho on Gerrard's
decision to stay at Liverpool

Can't Buy Gerrard
(Can't Buy Me Love)

Sung to Chelsea after they failed
in their bid to sign Steven Gerrard

Can't buy Gerrard
Can't buy Gerrard
Can't buy Gerrard
Money can't buy Gerrard

You think you got the most of things
But you ain't got Stevie G
Cause we're the Kop and we've got pride
And we've got history
We don't need your f*cking money
Cause we've got Stevie G

Can't buy Gerrard
Can't buy Gerrard
Can't buy Gerrard
Money can't buy Gerrard

'He is our talisman - I mean you just can't replace him. Thank goodness everything was sorted out last year! Everything's settled down now and I know he wil be with us for life. He's an unbelievable player and I wouldn't swap him for anyone. He has go everything and never ceases to amaze. He has been magnificent, different class.'

LFC Chairman
David Moores on Steven Gerrard

Istanbul (Amarillo)

Looking forward to the 5th EC/CL victory

When the day is dawning
On a Scouser's Sunday morning
How I long to be there
With the Cup that's waiting for me there

Every lonely T*ffee
La, la, la, la, la
Who's never won f*ck
Aint half as pretty
As the European Cup

Is this the way to Istanbul
Every night I've been on the road dreaming
Dreaming dreams of Istanbul
And the Cup that waits for me
Sha la, la, la, la, la, la, la
Sha la, la, la, la, la, la, la
Sha la, la, la, la, la, la, la
And the Cup that waits for me

'It was reported that we'd have 20,000 fans out here but there was much more than that. They are unbeliev-able and I dedicate this victory to them.'

Steven Gerrard after
winning the Champions League

He Missed From Two Yards
(Sloop John B)

Sung to Chelsea striker Andrei Shevchenko
following his point blank shot which was
saved by Jerzy Dudek and his penalty miss
in the CL Final 2005 whilst playing for Milan

He missed from two yards
He missed from two yards
In Istanbul
He missed from two yards

He missed from twelve yards
He missed from twelve yards
In Istanbul
He missed from twelve yards

'It is one of the greatest finals of all time and the save Jerzy Dudek made from Shevchenko at the end was unbelievable. I can't believe we've won. He'll be a legend now, not just for the penalties but because o the Shevchenko saves in the game itself. They were unbelievable.'

Jamie Carragher on Jerzy Dudek.

A Big Pole In Our Goal (He's Got The Whole World In His Hands)

Tribute to Jerzy Dudek

We've got a big Pole in our goal
We've got a great big Pole in our goal
We've got a big Pole in our goal
We've got a big Pole in our goal

'Carra came up to me after extra time and said 'Remember Grobbelaar and the rubbery legs of 84 - and do the same. Dance, do anything, put them off!'

Jerzy Dudek after his
penalty saving heroics in Istanbul

The Cup's In Its Liverpool Home

Sung in bars in Turkey after the CL Final 2005

Maldini scored first and he gave us a fright
We went three nil down and they thought we were sh*te
But we won the Cup for the fifth time that night
The Cup's in its Liverpool home

'This is without doubt my biggest night in football. At half-time we needed to do something and decided to make some changes. The early goal helped and with the backing of our wonderful supporters we went on from there. There is no way we could have went back out and lost by four or five goals in front of them.'

Rafael Benitez after winning the EC

We Won It Five Times
(Sloop John B)

Tribute to the fifth European Cup Win at the
Attaturk Stadium in Istanbul

We won it at Wembely
We won in Gay Paris
In 77 and 84 it was Rome

We've won it five times
We've won it five times
In Istanbul
We won it five times

When Emlyn lifted it high
He lit up the Roman sky
Thommo in Paris
And Souness did it as well

We've won it five times
We've won it five times
In Istanbul
We won it five times

Stevie G's eyes lit up
As he lifted the Euro Cup
Twenty one years and now it's coming back home

We've won it five times
We've won it five times
In Istanbul
We won it five times

'I wanted to show everybody that I'm still a good footballer, that I still have something to say. I think I have succeeded with that goal and that penalty. It wasn't a nice view at half time, but we wanted to get a goal for our fans as we didn't want them to be sad. I'm spellbound by it all, this is maybe the greatest moment in my career.'

Vladimir Smicer after Istanbul

Oh Istanbul

Sung in bars across Istanbul ahead of
and after the 05/06 CL Final

Oh Istanbul (oh Istanbul)
Is wonderful (is wonderful)
Oh Istanbul is wonderful
It's full of mosques, kebabs and Scousers
Oh Istanbul is wonderful

'...it was the Liverpool supporters who played their part so magnificently. From the sound and noise of half-time you would never have known it was Liverpool who were three down in Europe's showpiece final and Jamie Carragher was quick to go over to the fans at the final whistle and thank their '12th man'. I do not think you would find the fans of many clubs staying so vociferous in such trying circumstances.'

Mark Lawrenson after the Final at the Attaturk

Its Only On Loan (Sloop John B)

Looking ahead to the 06/07 Champions League

It's only on loan
It's only on loan
In ancient Greece
We'll bring it back home

'We gave everything but it wasn't to be tonight and certainly this feels the complete opposite to what it was like after Istanbul.'

Steven Gerrard after
losing the 06/07 Final to Milan

You F*cked It Up

Sung to the Luton fans after Liverpool came
from 3-1 down to win 5-3 in the 05/06 FA Cup

Three one, and you f*cked it up
Three one, and you f*cked it up
Three one, and you f*cked it up
Three one, and you f*cked it up
(Repeat as necessary)

'I never thought we'd lost the game yesterday, not even when there was only five minutes left and not even when we went into injury time. When you have the best player in the world in your side then you know that anything is possible. I was just praying for somebody to do something special and Stevie came up trumps again.'

Djibril Cisse after the 05/06 FA Cup win over West Ham

Fowler's Prayer (The Lord's Prayer)

Being thankful for the return of 'God'

Our Fowler
Thou art is scoring
Robbie be thy name
Thy transfer be done
On a free as it is in January
Give us this day our favourite Red
Alonso will give you the passes
As Carra' stops those who pass against us
Deliver us the title
And lead us not into relegation
For eleven is your number
Forever and ever
Our man

'Honest to God, I'm so happy it's frightening!
I'm just so chuffed - that's all I can say. Obviously
since I have left, deep down I have always wanted
to come back and it has been a long time but
I'm glad to say I'm back now.'

Robbie Fowler on
his return to Anfield

A Long Way Back To Chelsea
(A Long Way To Tippperary)

Celebrating the 2-1 06/07 Community Shield Win

Oh it's a long way back to Chelsea
It's a long way to go
It's a long way back to Chelsea
For Jose Mourinho

Up the M62
Down the M6 and M1
Oh it's a long way back to Chelsea
When your team's been beat 2-1

'This Is Anfield' means everything. You're so proud when you actually walk out, up the steps, and see it. Shankly said it was for the opposition, that it worries them; but I think it gives our players confidence. It's an absolutely incredible feeling when you're walking down the tunnel.'

Ian Rush

On The March With Rafa's Army
(My Old Man's A Dustman)

After finding out the 06/07 FA Cup Final will be
played at the Millennium Stadium…..again

On the March with Rafa's army
We'll win the FA Cup
The game won't be at Wembley
'Cos the builders f*cked it up
So take us back to Cardiff
It don't matter where we play
'Cos we're with Rafa's army and we'll win it anyway

'It was a great final, which is good for the competition after the way some people have derided it. Being a defender, I would have rather it had been 1-0 - but it was great for everyone to watch.'

Jamie Carragher after the 05/06 FA Cup Final

You Aint Got No History

A song that can often be heard in recent times
after Chelsea began bragging about their successes
following the Abramovich takeover

F*ck off Chelsea F.C
You aint got no history
Five European Cups
And eighteen Leagues
That's what we call history

'When I see the Bill Shankly statue, I look at the senti-
ment on the base. It says: 'He made the people happy'.
Well now the modern Liverpool is making the fans
and the city happy. And that makes me so proud.'

Gerard Houllier

John Arne Riise (Hey Baby)

One of the most popular songs on Merseyside,
given that the left sided defender/midfielder not
only scores all the time, but only seems to do
so from twenty yards or more

John Arne Riise (ooh-ah)
I wanna knooow
How'd you score that goal?

'We always work hard at Liverpool, but there are exciting times ahead and everyone wants to be part of that. They want to be part of the future here.'

John Arne Riise on the future of Liverpool

Kuyt, Kuyt (The Lord of the Dance)

A homage to Dutch striker Dirk
Kuyt following his decision to join
Liverpool despite interest from others

Kuyt, Kuyt wherever you may be
Dutch Kopite not a smug Geordie
It could be w*nk
You could be a Manc
Or a Chelski blue with old fat Frank

Kuyt, Kuyt wherever you may be
Hit every branch on the ugly tree
And with Fowler, Crouch and Craig Bellamy
Dirk Kuyt's boss but he's f*cking ugly

'I only wanted to leave Feyenoord for a really big club, and that is what Liverpool are. They are a fantastic, big club and it will be a real pleasure to play here.'

Dirk Kuyt on joining Liverpool

Luis Garcia (You Are My Sunshine)

A song for the diminutive Spaniard, heard many times
in the league and on the road to Istanbul

Luis Garcia
He drinks sangria
He came from Barca
To bring us joy
He's four foot seven
He's football heaven
Oh please don't take our Luis away

'A football club isn't just made up of players, coaches and directors. More than anything else it's the supporters who make a club, and that perhaps is the ingredient which best distinguishes Liverpool Football Club from every other team. The supporters. Because if one thing has remained obvious to me after these few years, it's that with supporters like you, Liverpool Football Club will never walk alone.'

Luis Garcia after leaving Liverpool for Atletico Madrid

We've Got The Best Midfield In The World (The Entertainer)

Praise for just some of the 07/08 season midfield players

Oh, oh, oh
We've got the best midfield in the world
With Xabi Alonso
Momo Sissoko
Gerrard and Mascherano oh, oh

'To work hard and have our supporters behind us and believing until the end, you run a little bit more'

Rafael Benitez

There Was A Local Derby
(The Laughing Policeman)

The T*ffee's get it. Again

There was a local derby
Not too long ago
The Evert*n fans were singing
Howard Kendall he must go
But then he won a trophy
And he was Evert*n's pride
You two faced Evert*n b*stards
You're the sh*te of Merseyside

Oh ha, ha, ha, ha, ha, ha, ha, ha, ha, ha, ha, ha, hah

There was a local derby
Not too long ago
The Evert*n fans were singing
All the songs they know
Just when Kenny scored a goal
They said it was offside
But we don't care cos' they scored none
And we scored f*cking five

Oh ha, ha, ha, ha, ha, ha, ha, ha, ha, ha, ha, ha, hah

There was a local derby
Not too long ago
The Evert*n fans were singing
David Moyes he must go
But then he finished fourth
And he was Evert*n's pride
You two faced Evert*n b*stards
You're the sh*te of Merseyside

Oh ha, ha, ha, ha, ha, ha, ha, ha, ha, ha, ha, ha, hah

'When you see the supporters and how the club works it is like a religion to them. We will try to do our best to bring more trophies back for them.'

Rafael Benitez

Follow, Follow, Follow

Looking forward to more domestic and European
success. And of course a pop at Man Utd never
goes amiss either

Follow, follow, follow
As Liverpool go to Europe
There'll be thousands of Reds
All pissed off their heads
As Liverpool go to Europe

Follow, follow, follow
As Liverpool win the League
The Manc's are in bed
All crying instead
As Liverpool win the League

'He couldn't play anyway. I only wanted him
for the reserve team!'

Bill Shankly upon hearing Celtic's Lou
Macari had snubbed Liverpool in
favour of a move to Manchester United

Harry Kewell (Quartermasters Stores)

Homage to the injury plagued Australian
Winger via a dig at the country's past

He's Red, he's white
His Grandpa stole me bike
Harry Kewell
Harry Kewell

He's Red, he's lame
He barely gets a game
Harry, Harry Kewell

'When I arrived at Liverpool, I brought with me the memory of once seeing Harry play against Manchester United for Leeds at Old Trafford and he was fantastic.'

Rafael Benitez on Harry Kewell

Going Loco With Momo Sissoko
(Going Loco Down In Acapulco)

Praise for central midfielder Mohamed Sissoko

We'll be going loco with Momo Sissoko
Cos he's big and strong
Yeah we'll be going loco with Momo Sissoko
This lad just can't do no wrong

Feel the pressure
Your back's against the wall
With Momo on your heels you'll never get the ball

Cos we'll be going loco with Momo Sissoko
Cos he's big and strong
Yeah we'll be going loco with Momo Sissoko
This lad just can't do no wrong

'Some of my staff came to me at the end of the game and said they thought Momo would have been their man-of-the-match as well as Steven Gerrard. Maybe a lot of people don't recognise how important Momo is, but everyone at the club knows it.'

Rafael Benitez heaps praise on
Sissoko after the 05/06 FA Cup Final

Agger Do (Agga Do)

Homage to Danish centre back Daniel Agger

Agger doo, doo, doo
Plays with Carra or Sami
Agger doo, doo, doo
Plays for Liverpool F.C

He can shoot
He can score
From thirty yards like Stevie G
Agger doo, doo, doo
Plays for Liverpool F.C

Agger doo, doo, doo
Since we signed him from Brondby
Agger doo, doo, doo
Plays for Liverpool F.C

To the left
To the right

He brings strikers to their knee's
Agger doo, doo, doo
Plays for Liverpool F.C

'To have played fifty times for Liverpool by the age of twenty two shows the quality he has. He has the potential to be up there with the likes of Hansen and Smith, and that's an accolade of the highest order.'

Gary Gillespie on Daniel Agger

A Team Of Carraghers
(Yellow Submarine)

More praise for centre back Jamie Carragher

We all dream of a team of Carraghers
A team of Carraghers
A team of Carraghers

Number one is Carragher
Number two is Carragher
Number three is Carragher
Number four is Carragher, Carragher

We all dream of a team of Carraghers
A team of Carraghers
A team of Carraghers

Number five is Carragher
Number six is Carragher
Number seven is Carragher
Number eight is Carragher, Carragher

We all dream of a team of Carraghers
A team of Carraghers
A team of Carraghers

Number nine is Carragher
Number ten is Carragher
Number eleven is Carragher
And twenty three is Carragher

We all dream of a team of Carraghers
A team of Carraghers
A team of Carraghers

'I went so mad that I must have had a bit of a blackout. I just crashed to the floor somewhere and I can't remember a single thing that was going on around me for a few moments. What I do remember as I was lying on the floor was starting to cramp up again!'

Jamie Carragher after the 05/06 EC Final

He's Big, He's Red
(Quartermasters Stores)

Homage to the 6'7 striker and his
'Robokop' goal celebration

He's big
He's Red
His feet stick out the bed
Peter Crouch, Peter Crouch

He's Red
He's mad
He dances like your dad
Peter Crouch, Peter Crouch

'Once I heard of their interest in me it was hard not to think about what it would be like to pull on the famous Red shirt and play in front of the Kop...'

Peter Crouch on his decision to join Liverpool

Crouch, Crouch
(Lord Of The Dance)

A song for the lofty striker during the
06/07 European Cup run

Crouch, Crouch
Wherever you may be
You didn't stop at six foot three
But you're not just tall
You're a master on the ball
And you'll win us the cup when we get to Greece

'He's fantastic on the ground but he's
obviously really tall'

Michael Owen tells it like it is

Fernando (Fernando)

Welcome to Anfield for new striker Fernando Torres

There was something in the air tonight
The smell of fright, Fernando
'Cos now they know you've come to Merseyside
They run and hide, Fernando

And with you and Crouchie in attack
We'll have the title back Fernando.
So tell the Manc's that they can f*ck off home
Their time has come, Fernando

'My challenge is to triumph in Liverpool and become the best striker in the club's history. I know that this will be difficult, but I am prepared for the adventure.'

Fernando Torres sets his sights high

Can't Take The Ball Off Of You
(Can't Take My Eyes Off You)

Another one for Stevie G

You're just too good to be Blue
Can't take the ball off of you
You've got a heavenly touch
You pass like Souness to Rush
And when we're pissed in the bars
We all thank God that you're ours
You're just too good to be Blue
Can't take the ball off of you

Oh Steven Gerrard
Because you're Red and white
Oh Steven Gerrard
Because you hate the sh*te
Oh Steven Gerrard
Trust in us in when we say

Oh Steven Gerrard
Because you hate Man U
Oh Steven Gerrard
You hate the Blue sh*te too
Oh Steven Gerrard,
You're a Red through and through

'I'd put Steven in the top five or six players in the world. In my opinion, I would say he was probably the best. I don't think anyone else could play for Liverpool and do more than he does.'

Jamie Carragher on Steven Gerrard

Torres On A Run
(Seasons In The Sun)

One of the many new songs being sung
about the Spanish hitman

Goodbye to you Utd scum
We want our title back your time has come
And now that Rafa's got it right
We'll beat you all 'cos you're all sh*te
You've got no place in the top flight

We've got joy, we've got fun
We've got Torres on a run
And he'll never be stopped
'Cos he's playin' for the Kop

'On Saturday I realised how to be a hero at Anfield. The people were happy with my goals and it was a sensational experience.'

Fernando Torres following the 07/08 6-0 demolition of Derby County

Stevie G (Let It Be)

In true Liverpool style, another Beatles song is
adapted for one of the Kop's greatest heroes

When we find ourselves in times of trouble
Stevie G runs past me
Playing the game with wisdom
Stevie G
And in my home the Spion Kop
I watch him jog in front of me
Spreading balls with wisdom
Stevie G

Let it be, let it be, let it be, Stevie G
The local lad turned hero
Stevie G

And when the jubilant Kopite people
All living in The Park agree
That we all know the answer
Stevie G
And although we may all be fooled
There is still a chance that we will see
The greatest football genius
Stevie G

Let it be, let it be, let it be, Stevie G
Spreading balls with wisdom
Stevie G

And when the night is cloudy
There is still a man that we all see
A young, committed Kopite
Stevie G
Playing to the sound of music
Stevie G runs past me
Playing the game with wisdom
Stevie G

Let it be, let it be, let it be, Stevie G
For we all know the answer
Stevie G

'He's been influential for Liverpool over the years and has changed games and won European Cups by himself…Now he's doing that for England so it's great for us.'

England Manager Steve Mclaren on **Steven Gerrard**

Sami Hyypia (The Addams Family)

Praise for the enormous defender

In our defensive foursome
He's absolutely awesome
From corners he will score some
It's Sami Hyypia

'Everyone talks about foreign players like Zola, Henry and Bergkamp but they never look at Sami. In terms of consistency he's well up there with them, there's no doubt about it. Maybe he can do something out of the blue every now and again but every week, for nine months of the season, Sami Hyypia is your man. He's definitely one of the best foreign players this country has ever seen.'

Jamie Carragher on Sami Hyypia

Rafa, Rafael (Skip To The Lou)

Praise for the Spanish Coach

We've got a coach from Spain
He will make us great again
That is why we sing his name
Rafael Benitez
Rafa, Rafael
Rafa, Rafael
Rafa, Rafael
Rafael Benitez

'What Rafa has done this season surpasses, without any doubt, what any other manager has done. Jose Mourinho has won the league for Chelsea in his first season and made a real impact in England. But it doesn't come even close to winning the European Cup in your first season. Now Rafa can go and tell any press conference he likes, as Jose did, that he's the true champion. Mourinho can't say that any more. So is Rafa the special one too? Well, he is to Liverpool fans.'

Jamie Carragher on Rafael Benitez

Rafa's Got His Dirk Out

More praise and a cheeky play on words for the
hard working Dutch Forward

Rafa's got his Dirk out
Rafa's got his Dirk out
Da, da, da, da
Da, da, da, da
Rafa's got his Dirk out
Rafa's got his Dirk out
Da, da, da, da
Da, da, da, da

'The crowd has been incredible to me from the first moment of my debut against West Ham. The minute I stepped on to the pitch, I felt I had been a Liverpool player for a long time'

Dirk Kuyt

Oh One Man United

A song to remind Man Utd who's really the best in
England. And Evert*n don't escape either

Oh one Man Utd
Oh one football team
Oh one Old Trafford
Where they like to dream

But over in Anfield
Reality reigns
With Five European Cups
Alongside our name

And eighteen League Titles
We're ahead of the rest
Just look round our trophy room
To see we're best

But over in Goodison
No cups will be seen
Unless having lunch
In the players canteen

'Rafa has the feel of this club, he knows the history of the club and he loves the people. I tell you what, we have got a good man.'

Liverpool Chairman
David Moores on Rafael Benitez

Steve Gerrard, Gerrard (Que Sera)

Guaranteed to be heard from almost every supporter
whenever the skipper is on the pitch

Steve Gerrard, Gerrard
He'll pass the ball forty yards
He's big and he's f*ckin' hard
Steve Gerrard, Gerrard

(variation)

Steve Gerrard, Gerrard
He scores 'em from forty yards
He hits 'em so f*ckin' hard
Steve Gerrard, Gerrard

Y.N.W.A